THERESA A. WHELPLEY

UNMASKING THE SPIRITS

REVIEW AND HERALD PUBLISHING ASSOCIATION
WASHINGTON, D.C. 20012

Copyright © 1977 by the
Review and Herald Publishing Association
Library of Congress Catalog Card No. 74-20471

Editor: Thomas A. Davis
Cover: Jim Burtnett
Book Design: Alan Forquer

Oringal Publication Date: 1977

Reprint Publication Date: 2021

The content of this book is presented as it was originally published and should be read with its original publication date in mind.

ISBN: 978-0-8127-0531-7

Printed in U.S.A.

CONTENTS

Ouija Boards and Telegraph Keys	5
Revival of Spiritism	13
I Was a Spiritist	23
Can the Dead Talk With the Living?	30
Are the Spirits Angels?	34
"Chains You Can Never Break"	43
The Witch of Endor	50
Can the Spirits Predict the Future?	56
Body, Soul, and Spirit	61
Is Man's Soul Immortal?	68
Spiritism Is Not Christian	75

1

OUIJA BOARDS AND TELEGRAPH KEYS

Jabez Pendleton Billings was the manager of a summer resort a few miles from Lyons, Colorado. The resort was owned by a Mrs. Arbuckle.

One day Jabez and Mrs. Arbuckle's nephew were surveying some unmapped land above Estes Park, which was uninhabited at the time. As they made their way along a narrow trail at the top of an embankment, the nephew suddenly slipped and fell down the embankment, breaking a leg.

With the aid of the walking stick Jabez threw him, the injured man managed to get to where Jabez could help him crawl painfully and with great difficulty back to the trail. Supported by Mr. Billings and the stick, Mrs. Arbuckle's nephew slowly made his way to where help could be had.

It was late afternoon when the men finally reached an inhabited section where there was a telephone. When they left home they had told

Mrs. Arbuckle that they would be back at a certain time, which had long passed. Thinking that she would be anxious, Jabez telephoned to explain the reason for their delay.

But before he could say a word by way of explanation, Mrs. Arbuckle interrupted, "Don't tell me. Let me tell you what my ouija board told me."

She went on to describe in detail how her nephew had slipped on the narrow path, fallen down the embankment, broken his leg, and, with the aid of Mr. Billings and his walking stick, had crawled back onto the trail.

Then she told Jabez that, after the two of them had left home, she had begun playing with the ouija. Suddenly, to her amazement, it began to spell out the story she related to Jabez. But how could the ouija do that?

While waiting one day for a haircut in the neighborhood barber shop, my father got into a conversation with another customer about spirit messages. The young man, whose name was Fraser, claimed that he had even rigged up a telegraph system by which the spirits communicated with him. My father and Jack Keleher, the barber, expressed doubts, so the man invited them to his house.

"Come over some evening and I will prove to you that it is not a fake," he said. Out of curiosity my father and Mr. Keleher went.

After asking questions that were answered by knocks on the table or through the ouija board, Mr. Fraser introduced his telegraph equipment. He would ask a question and the answer would be spelled out on the key of the machine, which Mr. Fraser wrote out.

My father, who knew of spiritualistic experiences others of his family had had, was still unconvinced. He was sure that it was simply a sleight-of-hand performance, and that Fraser himself worked the telegraph key.

Finally the spiritist said, "One of you ask me a question you are sure I can't answer."

Mr. Keleher thought a moment. "Where did Jim Mahoney stable his horses when he went to town?"

That would stump Fraser, Mr. Keleher was sure. Farmer Mahoney was an old man when the barber himself was a boy. The spiritist could not possibly have known him.

Eagerly Mr. Keleher and my father watched as Mr. Fraser wrote out the answer that came, giving the street name and precise number where the stable, long torn down, had stood.

The two men were astonished and baffled, but still not satisfied. "All right, don't take my word for it," said Mr. Fraser. "You can talk with the spirits yourselves, just as I do." He went on to explain how that could be done.

The Keleher family and ours were good

friends. One evening when my parents came home from a visit to the Kelehers they exclaimed excitedly as they came through the door, "We did it!"

"Did what?" I asked.

"We got the table moving like Fraser said we could. We never dreamed we could do it, but we did!" Father was aglow with excitement.

Unknown to me, they had been carrying out the medium's instructions at the Keleher home. Night after night my parents, Mr. and Mrs. Keleher, their daughter, Bertha, and her husband sat on the same chairs with their hands spread out on spots they had marked on the table. There in the darkened room they silently waited to see if the spirits would communicate with them.

Nothing happened the first few evenings. Then one night they heard a knock. Each looked at the others, sure that one of them had rapped the table for a joke. At the next meeting not only was there knocking but also the table started to sway. The following evening there was no doubt about it; the table rocked, raised off the floor, and moved about the room.

"You should have seen it! You must come down and see it tomorrow night," Father said as he removed his coat.

"I don't want to go down. I don't want anything to do with it," I replied. "I will not put myself under its influence."

"You don't have to put yourself under any influence. You need not even sit at the table if you don't want to. Elizabeth [one of the Keleher daughters] wasn't there and she wants to see it. She doesn't want to sit at the table, so the two of you can sit off to one side."

My parents insisted, so I gave in and went down. Elizabeth and I sat in a corner of the room while the six participants sat around the table, their hands spread out on the same marked spots as they had been the other evenings.

I felt strangely out of place as I sat there in that darkened room, and I wished I had not come. I remembered an experience my mother had had some time before. A friend had lost her diamond ring and, unable to find it, decided to seek the help of a spiritist. The medium would not have a "sitting" unless there were ten persons present, so Mother was asked to help make up the number.

The women sat quietly while the spiritist endeavored to contact the spirits. She tried and tried but could not get through. Finally she said, "There is someone here who is not in harmony and who has an opposing spirit, so the spirits will not come." Then, pointing to one of the women, she asked her to leave the room, saying, "I cannot do a thing while she is present." After the woman left, the medium made contact with the spirits and told Mother's friend where the ring could be found. When Mother told me of the experience I was impressed that there was something unusal about it.

Now, waiting silently in the shadows, I did not want to get involved, so I prayed that God would not let anything happen. We sat there for more than an hour without speaking a word. It was very silent and the time dragged slowly. During all that time there was not a sound, a knock, nor a movement of the table.

The group couldn't understand it. "Why, we had the table moving all over the place last night," commented Bertha. "When it got to going too fast, we had to move lively to keep up with it so we could keep our hands on it as it swung about from one side of the room to the other."

Now I was more convinced than ever that I wanted nothing to do with it, because, in answer to my prayer, God had taken control and demonstrated that He was stronger than the spirits.

By this time my parents' curiosity was satisfied; they did not pursue spiritism any further.

Everyone who honestly investigates spiritism and phases of the occult with a degree of thoroughness comes to the place where he has to admit that there is a supernatural power involved. It is true that spiritists have used sleight-of-hand methods to deceive, and mass hypnotism can make people see things that do not exist. But there are some things that cannot be explained by trickery that prove there is an intelligence back of it.

It is unusual experiences such as these that lead thousands of people to examine spiritism and the occult. This is especially so after losing a loved one. How the bereaved wish they could contact the departed and ask him questions!

The late Bishop Pike became interested in spiritism because he believed he received messages from his son, Jim, who had committed suicide. And after the death of his mother Dr. Norman Vincent Peale claimed he communicated with her.

But various texts of Scripture indicate that the dead do not return. For example:

Job 16:22: "When a few years are come, then I shall go the way whence I shall not return."

Job 7:9, 10: "He that goeth down to the grave shall come up no more. He shall return no more to his house, neither shall his place know him any more."

2 Kings 22:20: "I will gather thee unto thy fathers [said God], and thou shalt be gathered into thy grave in peace; and thine eyes shall not see all the evil which I will bring upon this place."

If, as the Bible says, the dead do not come back, and have no knowledge of what is taking place on the earth, whoever it was that gave the information about where the long-dead Farmer Mahoney stabled his horses, it was not Farmer Mahoney. Then who did spell out the very number and name of the street where he stabled his horses when he went shopping in town? The spiritist had never heard of him and the stable had long since disappeared. But someone knew the farmer's habits and reported them to the medium through the telegraph system. And who reported to Mrs. Arbuckle every detail of her nephew's accident and his rescue?

REVIVAL OF SPIRITISM

Today there seems to be an accelerated reaching out after something beyond the seen and known. Men are exploring outer space and delving into the depths of the sea. Millions are experimenting with drugs in order to experience new sensations and to get away from reality. In spiritism, witchcraft, astrology, hypnosis, telepathy, and all forms of mysticism there is a revival of ancient practices that are forbidden in the Bible.

Through Moses, God instructed Israel: "There shall not be found among you any one . . . that useth divination, or an observer of times, or an enchanter, or a witch, or a charmer, or a consulter with familiar spirits, or a wizard, or a necromancer. For all that do these things are an abomination unto the Lord" (Deut. 18:10-12).

During the first half of the nineteenth century some of these ancient arts came into new prominence in what is called spiritism. One group among which it developed was the Shakers, an offshoot of the Quakers. In 1774 a woman, Ann Lee, emigrated from England with seven or eight companions. Later, her followers set up communes in New York State and New England.

The Shakers came to believe that Ann Lee was the divine "Mother" through whom Christ's Spirit made a second appearing. Between the years 1837 and 1847 the group in New Lebanon, New York, professed to talk with the dead and particularly to receive instructions from their deceased leader. The group at Alfred, Maine, practiced spiritualistic healings.

A prominent spiritist of the nineteenth century was Andrew Jackson Davis, who was born in Orange County, New York, in 1826. He became interested in hypnotism, or mesmerism as it was then known, and claimed to receive spiritualistic messages concerning his lifework. For a number of years he practiced as a healer. Although he had little education, he wrote a number of volumes, most of which he dictated while in a trance.

The Swedenborgians, or the New Jerusalem Church, which spread from England to America in the early 1800's, developed from the teachings of Emanuel Swedenborg, a Swedish scientist, philosopher, and mystic (1688-1772). Some students of spiritism believe that modern spiritism sprang from Swedenborg. He delved into the spiritual side of life and devoted his time to intercourse with the spiritual world. He had visions and dreams and claimed to have conversations with angels and spirits as well as with his deceased friends and great men of antiquity. He wrote voluminously on his findings.

We usually think of modern spiritism as starting with the Fox sisters in 1848. When the Fox family moved into a house in the township of Hydesville, New York, not far from Rochester, they heard strange noises that they could not identify but that caused them considerable annoyance. Finally the youngest daughter, Kate,* challenged the mysterious rappings. "Here, old Splitfoot," she called, alluding to the devil, as she snapped her fingers, "do this!" She expected no reply, so was startled when the same number of snapping sounds came back. She tried it again and again and was soon receiving answers to her questions. Kate, and later her sister, Margaret, claimed to be in communication with the spirits of the dead.

At first people were skeptical. But after investigations were made they had to admit there was something superhuman about what was happening. Others became interested and the movement spread rapidly.

---

* Accounts differ as to whether it was Catherine (known as Kate or Katie) or Margeretta (also known as Margaret and Maggie) who first communicated with the spirits.

Soon unusual phenomena followed. Musical instruments were played without any visual contact. Tables moved and sometimes rose from the floor and floated through the air. Spirit messages were written on slates. At times spirit forms seemed to appear. A spirit would dip its hand into hot paraffin, disappear, and leave behind it a paraffin glove.

Among the first professional mediums were a Mrs. W. R. Hayden and Daniel D. Home. Both practiced in England, but came from the United States. Home was able to practice levitation, a phenomenon in which his body rose from the floor and floated about without visible support. Naturally, such demonstrations attracted much attention. Today there are some 1,500 registered spiritist mediums in the United States alone.

Fake clairvoyants, fortunetellers and mediums, seeking to gain fame or easy money, or both, began to imitate these mysterious manifestations, with the result that scientists ignored spiritism, and it fell into disrepute. Also, churches condemned spiritism. But in time it began to make a comeback and to move into high society. After World War I it became known that at least some of the crowned heads of Europe consulted spiritist mediums in regard to the pursuit of the war.

Adolph Hitler was believed to have governed Nazi Germany and carried on World War II with the aid of astrology. It is reported that, not to be outdone, the British Secret Service used astrologers to study Hitler's horoscope to find out what his astrologers were advising him. It is reported that the queen of England still maintains an astrologer royal.

It is known that some United States Presidents have sought counsel from spiritists. On at least two occasions President Franklin D. Roosevelt consulted Jeane Dixon and her crystal ball about the war and our relationship with Soviet Russia.

The late president of Haiti, François Duvalier, was a Catholic, but he was also a devout believer in voodoo. He is reported to have said, "Voodoo is not superstition. It is a philosophy, a conception of God."

Today, scientists are interested in the area of the occult. In fact, some universities are granting Ph.D.'s for research theses into the occult. Since the 1930's the Institute of Parapsychology at Duke University, Durham, North Carolina, has been researching the subject, especially extrasensory perception, or ESP, in an effort to discover its secrets. Scientists at the university are investigating case histories of people who have had unusual experiences that cannot be explained, such as a premonition of danger or death of a loved one, which premonition was later discovered to have been fulfilled as sensed just at the time it came.

Some universities, such as the universities of New York, South Carolina, and Alabama, as well as some high schools, offer courses in witchcraft that are well attended.

In many major cities witchcraft covens (circle of 13 members) meet regularly. On one recent occasion several thousand witches gathered in the Hollywood Bowl for a "Witchcraft Festival," described by *Newsweek* as the "world's largest spell cast to increase sexual vitality."

Jeane Dixon is no doubt the most noted of modern seers. Three million copies of a book about her, *A Gift of Prophecy,* have been sold. From childhood she has had an uncanny ability to predict future events. As early as 1952 she foretold that a tall young Democrat with blue eyes and thick brown hair would be elected to the presidency of the United States in 1960 and would meet death by violence while in office.

And on the fateful day of November 22, 1963, while dining with friends in the Mayflower Hotel, Washington, D.C., she could not eat because she knew that was the day. During the meal, the announcement was made that John Kennedy had been shot. Then she recalled a fleeting vision in which she saw the name of the assassin and remembered that it was a five- or six-letter name with two syllables. The first letter was "O" or "Q" and the second definitely an "S." The man accused of committing the crime, Lee Harvey Oswald, fitted the description.

While still a child, Jeane Dixon foretold the election of Herbert Hoover in 1928. She also predicted the four elections of Franklin Delano Roosevelt, as well as his death. She saw that Harry Truman would become President "by an act of God" and that he would serve a second term. She foretold the election of Dwight D. Eisenhower. Actually, many of her prophecies have failed, and she has altered her interpretation of some of her major prophecies. Nevertheless, some of her forecasts that have been fulfilled were of such a dramatic and public nature that she has become world famous.

For many centuries spiritism and all similar forms of psychic phenomena have been considered contrary to the teachings of both the Hebrew and Christian religions and have been denounced as evil. But in modern times they have taken on a religious garb. Many spiritist churches have sprung up. Sometimes spiritists hold public meetings in large auditoriums and halls that attract big crowds. The meetings may be opened by the singing of hymns and prayer, just as in a Christian church. Jeane Dixon, although a spiritist, is a very devout Catholic. Elsie England and Mrs. Whitney, who tell their stories in later chapters, both believed they were consecrated Christians doing God's service.

And more and more Protestant congregations are becoming involved in spiritism. Some have even set aside rooms where their members can communicate with their departed loved ones.

There are differences of opinion regarding what spiritism is, and its place in the church. Andrew M. Greeley, a Roman Catholic priest of the University of Chicago, writes, "What is going on is authentically, if perhaps transiently and bizarrely, religious; the new pursuit of the sacred." But a spokesman for the Catholic Information Center in Washington, D.C., warned against taking up witchcraft and astrology. "Our advice to young people," he said, "is to stay away from it—it's dangerous."

Spiritism has spread faster in Europe than in America. In England the Anglican Church has been investigating it, as has also the General Assembly of the Church of Scotland. A Church of Scotland leader, Dr. Norman MacLean, reported, "The church decided that psychical research was not contrary to the teachings of the Christian faith and that members of the church were not forbidden to exercise their minds in this field."

Spiritist churches and healers are listed in the telephone books of major cities of the United States. The National Council of Churches has a knowledge of 400 spiritist churches, with a membership of approximately 150,000.

Many youth in America are endeavoring to read the future by means of tarot cards, a deck of twenty-two cards used in fortunetelling and for otherwise foretelling future events. Some use the *I Ching*, an ancient Chinese book of divination.

It is said that the majority of those who are investigating the occult are in the under-30 age group. No doubt there are various reasons for their interest: curiosity, the allure of the mysterious, the attraction of adventure. For some it seems to be a form of religion.

"It is paradoxical," writes Frank E. Gaebelein, "that in this age of science and education, credulous followers of Spiritualism, theosophy, astrology and other kinds of occultism number in the millions."

The ouija board also has had a revival. In a recent year two million ouija boards were sold.

Chaytor Mason, psychologist at the University of Southern California, considers the occult craze in this country "a sign of monumental insecurity." And Dr. Ari Kiev, head of the Cornell University program in social psychiatry, warns that the occult is very often "the breeding ground for psychosis."

We used to think of devil worship as being exclusive to what we called heathen lands, but today in the "enlightened" United States people are openly worshiping the devil. From the Cathedral of the Fallen Angel in Los Angeles and the Church of Satan in San Francisco, the cult is spreading across the land.

Black masses are held in rooms painted black, where such items as black candles, skulls, daggers, toads, and crosses hung upside down are in evidence. It is claimed that nudity and sexual relations form a part of the worship in some of the services.

Devil possession, no longer confined—as was thought—to lands in spiritual darkness, seems to be multiplying in enlightened countries, where it was practically unheard of before.

It is reported that in England "priests are now finding all over the country that they are having to cast out devils and evil spirits." One priest in London carried out one thousand exorcisms (the casting out of devils) in two years. He attributes the increase to a greater interest in religion. People are reaching out for the supernatural and are dabbling in spiritism, fortunetelling, witchcraft, and black magic.

I WAS A SPIRITIST

(Elsie England, a former spiritist, tells her story.)
As a young girl, barely able to spell out words, I played with my grandma's ouija board. On one occasion, after I had tired of amusing myself by questions that were speedily answered, I asked who was answering the questions. Quickly the name "Satan" was spelled out. But because I did not know that was a name for the devil I just laughed to myself at the funny name—but I never forgot it.

I had always been considered a psychic. I could read fortunes from cards and tea leaves, and considered myself unusually gifted by the Lord. Never once did I consider that I was on the devil's playground, for I was actually a very religious child and wanted to obey the Lord.

As time went on, I progressed to actual séance spiritism, and the medium at the séances I attended always claimed she drew her strength while in her trance directly from me.

The medium was a housewife by the name of Kitty Henn. Her husband, Max, acted as host and led in the hymn singing, which supposedly "put her under." The eight or ten of us who attended would sit in darkness and quietly sing *a cappella* such old favorites as "Rock of Ages" until we would hear the characteristic sigh and heavy whispering sounds coming from Kitty. Following this, the spirits would come in strongly, particularly the ones whom we knew as the guides, who were usually, supposedly, Indians. Black Hawk, Kitty's favorite guide, grunted as we supposed Indian chiefs did, and announced himself, "Me Blackie Hawk." Our group, some of whom were public school teachers and other professional people, would sit in the dark for several hours communicating. Actually, much of the conversation with the spirits was pure twaddle meant to please those present. Nothing profound was discussed and I lost my patience many times because things like lost keys and house sales were delved into at great length. I could not understand people who had passed to a better place and who were "so happy" there paying such undue attention to petty things such as lost keys.

All manner of spirits came to my husband and me when we went to Kitty's—people who had died natural deaths and others who had committed suicide. These always came in whispering, "Please pray for me," which told us they had committed suicide. Their messages were usually brief, expressing their joy on the plane where they found themselves, and they made comments only if they were prodded.

Only one thing really troubled me. On the couple of occasions when I asked a spirit if it had seen Jesus, there was great, almost shocked, silence, and the medium immediately lost contact with her spirits and had to be sung back into her trance. I quickly realized that there was something wrong with mentioning the name of Jesus at a séance, but I had no idea why.

I had many interesting encounters with the professed spirits of familiar departed and was satisfied that life surely went on after death. One such experience concerned a young man named Gene, who was a merchant marine during World War II. He was killed in the Gulf of Mexico when his ship was torpedoed in American waters by a German submarine.

Gene was the son of my mother's best friend. When his mother heard the news and called mine to tell her about it I did not even know who was on the telephone. But when Mother said in horror, "Oh, no!" I distinctly heard the words "I didn't even know what hit me. I was down in the bottom of the ship when the torpedo hit." We afterward learned from his parents that survivors had confirmed the fact that he was down inside the vessel when it was hit.

Some time later the spirit purporting to be Gene, which now spoke to me frequently, asked me to get his guitar and give it to his brother, Sonny.

I didn't know Gene had a guitar. But the next time I visited his sister I asked her about it. She told me that he had played one. With that, the spirit spoke to me again. "My girl friend's got it. Mary has it. Tell her to get it from Mary and give it to Sonny. I want him to have it."

I asked his sister where the guitar was. She answered, "Gene's girl friend has it." When I asked her name, she told me it was Mary. Then the spirit indicated a westerly direction and said, "She lives over that way."

I questioned the sister about where Mary lived, and, sure enough, she pointed in a westerly direction. It was strange that the sister was not in the least surprised to hear me say, "Gene would like you to get the guitar from her and give it to Sonny."

The spirits finally moved right into my home in New York City and were with me all the time, manifesting themselves in unusual ways. One Christmas I trimmed a tree with small bells and assigned a particular bell to each familiar "departed spirit" so that I would know which one was trying to communicate with me. The bells would ring mysteriously with no apparent activators. This would shock my unsuspecting friends, but I took it matter-of-factly and with a great deal of interest.

One particular easy chair in our home was *un*easy for anyone sitting in it but me. It was in that chair that I received all my spirit messages, and any unsuspecting friend visiting for a while and sitting in that chair would bound out of it for no explainable reason.

After I had lost both my parents and young husband within two years, I was no longer able to go to the staged séances. But the spirits of what I thought to be my beloved dead talked to me all the time. In fact, my second marriage was a definite result of spiritism and a direct alliance with the devil himself. After my husband's untimely death at the age of 42, his "spirit" began immediately to talk to me directly. After my husband had been dead for some time and I expressed a terrible loneliness, the spirit assured me that he was "working on that right now. I am sending a man to you. You will know him when he tells you he was building himself a house."

On the very night my husband passed away, the man in question had been in the middle of the Atlantic Ocean aboard the *United States* attempting to commit suicide. He worked as a chef on that ship. He was the same height to the half-inch as my husband, weighed the same to the ounce, wore the same sized shoes and clothing, and was born the same day.

I was a choir member in our church. One Sunday morning, shortly after the spirit had told me to watch for a certain man who would use the identifying phrase "I was building myself a house," I was sitting in the choir loft. I noticed a tall, dark man walk down the aisle and sit in the pew where my husband had always sat. He took the very seat my husband had used and where nobody had sat since his death. I immediately had a feeling of resentment.

After the service, as I stood at the door with others to greet the visitors, this man walked directly up to me, shook my hand, told me his name, and added, "I have been fighting off an impulse to come to this church for the past three weeks and I really don't know what I'm doing here."

The following Wednesday night he came to prayer meeting, and I drove him to his apartment. As we sat talking in the car he suddenly said, "I was building myself a house——," then stopped abruptly, and said thoughtfully, "I wonder why I told you that. I have never spoken to anyone about it before."

I turned cold, for I knew that this was the man my husband had found for me. All my resistance melted, and with it my common sense. From that time Satan seemed to take full control of my life, and the next two years I would like to blot from my memory. At the end of the two years my new husband divorced me for being "too religious." He said he hated me because I had not quit praying for him since we were married.

Shortly after my divorce I was converted at the Seventh-day Adventist evangelistic center in New York, the New York Center, which is situated in the heart of an atheistic jungle. My conversion was immediate when I learned the true state of the dead and the entire Bible truth was made plain to me. From that day on I have had no spiritist experiences. I consider myself chosen and blessed of the Lord, for I surely had been among the lost ones when Christ rescued me.

CAN THE DEAD TALK WITH THE LIVING?

There are records of occasions when angels communicated with men. In the Bible, for example. If this is so, why shouldn't our loved ones, if they are conscious and go to heaven when they die, also talk with us? Let us see what answer the Scriptures give to this question.

God wants us to understand about the state of the dead, for under inspiration Paul wrote: "I would not have you to be ignorant, brethren, concerning them which are asleep, that ye sorrow not, even as others which have no hope" (1 Thess. 4:13). Here death is called a sleep, as it is in other places in the Bible. For instance, Psalm 13:3: "Lighten mine eyes, lest I sleep the sleep of death."

Jesus called death a sleep, as recorded in John 11:11-14: "He saith unto them, Our friend Lazarus sleepeth; but I go, that I may awake him out of sleep. Then said his disciples, Lord, if he sleep, he shall do well. Howbeit Jesus spoke of his death; but they thought that he had spoken of taking of rest in sleep. Then said Jesus unto them plainly, Lazarus is dead."

When a person is asleep he is unconscious of what is taking place about him. We read in Ecclesiastes 9:10: "Whatsoever thy hand findeth to do, do it with thy might; for there is no work, nor device, nor knowledge, nor wisdom, in the grave, whither thou goest." Verses five and six put it clearly: "True, the living know that they will die; but the dead know nothing. . . . For them love, hate, ambition, all are now over. Never again will they have any part in what is done here under the sun" (N.E.B.).

Psalm 146:4 tells us the dead do not think. "He breathes his last breath, he returns to the dust; and in that same hour all his thinking ends" (N.E.B.).

"For in death there is no remembrance of thee [God]: in the grave who shall give thee thanks?" "The dead praise not the Lord, neither any that go down into silence" (Ps. 6:5; 115:17).

Surely if the departed were in heaven living on a higher plane than they did on earth, they would remember God and praise Him for the blessings of eternal life in a sinless world. But, as we have seen, the Scriptures say that the dead have no remembrance of God and do not thank Him or praise Him.

Lazarus had been dead four days when Jesus

resurrected him. What a wonderful story Lazarus could have told had he spent those four days in heaven! What did he relate? Nothing! He was simply experiencing a state of unconsciousness that Jesus likened to sleep.

Recently, I met a woman who on one occasion had been pronounced dead by her doctors. But after six hours she suddenly revived to find plans being made for her funeral. When she awoke it was as if she had just fallen asleep. She knew nothing of the intervening hours.

Acts 2:29-34 are surprising texts: "Men and brethren, let me freely speak unto you of the patriarch David, that he is both dead and buried, and his sepulchre is with us unto this day. . . . For David is not ascended into the heavens." David died more than a thousand years before Peter preached his sermon on the day of Pentecost, but he had not yet gone to his reward in heaven.

According to Bible teaching, then, the dead have no mental processes—they have no concept of things around them, or of themselves, anymore than a sleeping person does—and they are not in heaven. If they are not in heaven, where are they?

"If I wait, the grave is mine house: I have made my bed in the darkness. . . . Our rest together is in the dust" (Job 17:13-16).

Christians believe in a general resurrection. But what would be the need of such a resurrection if people went to their reward as soon as they died? If they are already enjoying the pleasures of their heavenly home, what is the purpose of the resurrection? Will they go back into the grave to be resurrected?

Job gives an answer: "So man lieth down, and riseth not: till the heavens be no more, they shall not awake, nor be raised out of their sleep" (chap. 14:12).

After listing, in Hebrews 11, many people who through the ages had been victorious through faith, Paul closes the chapter with these words: "These also, one and all, are commemorated for their faith; and yet they did not enter upon the promised inheritance, because, with us in mind, God had made a better plan, that only in company with us should they reach their perfection" (verses 39, 40, N.E.B.).

"And this is the will of him that sent me [said Jesus], that every one which seeth the Son, and believeth on him, may have everlasting life: and I will raise him up at the last day" (John 6:40). So God plans to take all the righteous home together, at one time, when Jesus comes.

Thus, according to the Scriptures, it is not our departed loved ones who send back messages through the spiritist mediums, who slam doors, move furniture, and hurl things through the air. Then could they be angels? This is the question we shall discuss in the next chapter.

ARE THE SPIRITS ANGELS?

The Word of God has many stories of angels, both in the Old and the New Testaments. The work of angels is described by Paul in Hebrews 1:14: "Are they not all ministering spirits sent forth to serve, for the sake of those who are to obtain salvation?" (R.S.V.).

This work is referred to many times in the Bible: "The angel of the Lord encampeth round about them that fear him, and delivereth them" (Ps. 34:7). "Take heed that ye despise not one of these little ones; for I say unto you, That in heaven their angels do always behold the face of my Father which is in heaven" (Matt. 18:10).

Angels visited Abraham and Lot, and Cornelius, the Roman centurion, in the form of men (Gen. 18:1-8; 19:1-3, 15; Acts 10:1-3).

They protected the three young Hebrews in the fiery furnace (Dan. 3:24-28) and shut the mouths of the lions while Daniel spent the night in their den (chap. 6:22, 23). An angel delivered

Peter from prison (Acts 5:19; 12:7-11) and fed Elijah in the wilderness (1 Kings 19:5-8).

When our Saviour was physically and mentally exhausted from fasting forty days in the wilderness and battling temptation, and again after His agony in the Garden of Gethsemane, angels came and ministered to Him (Matt. 4:11; Luke 22:43). They also communicated God's will to man through the prophets. In Revelation 1:1 we read, "The Revelation of Jesus Christ, which God gave unto him, to show unto his servants things which must shortly come to pass; and he sent and signified it by his angel unto his servant John." So angels have very important duties to perform.

Some people believe that when human beings die they become angels. I remember as a child hearing people comment, when they saw a shooting star, "There goes a child up to heaven to become an angel."

But angels existed before anyone ever died on this earth. After Adam and Eve sinned they were driven from the Garden of Eden. "Therefore the Lord God sent him forth from the garden of Eden, to till the ground from whence he was taken. So he drove out the man; and he placed at the east of the garden of Eden Cherubims, and a flaming sword which turned every way, to keep the way of the tree of life" (Gen. 3:23, 24).

Inasmuch as angels appeared on this earth before anyone in the world had died, they could not be our loved ones who have passed away. They were created a separate, higher order of being. Speaking of man, the psalmist said, "For thou hast made him a little lower than the angels" (Ps. 8:5).

The Bible teaches that there are evil as well as good angels (Jude 6). The commander of the evil angels is called the devil, Satan (Rev. 12:9), and other names. We are warned, "Be sober, be vigilant; because your adversary the devil, as a roaring lion, walketh about, seeking whom he may devour" (1 Peter 5:8).

The devil was at one time a leading angel in heaven. Under the representation of the king of Tyre, the prophet Ezekiel reveals that Satan had been "the anointed cherub that covereth," which position is illustrated by the cherubim overshadowing the mercy seat in the Jewish sanctuary. Addressing him in the person of the king of Tyre, Ezekiel says, "Thou wast perfect in thy ways from the day that thou wast created, till iniquity was found in thee" (Eze. 28:14, 15). So Satan was created a perfect angel. How then did he become our adversary, the devil?

Verse 17 says, "Thine heart was lifted up because of thy beauty, thou hast corrupted thy wisdom by reason of thy brightness." The devil, then, is not a red monster with horns and hoofs and a forked tail, as he is often pictured. He was created a bright, beautiful angel who became exalted because of his beauty. Not only did he become proud but he also became ambitious.

"How art thou fallen from heaven, O Lucifer, son of the morning! how art thou cut down to the ground, which didst weaken the nations! For thou hast said in thine heart, I will ascend into heaven, I will exalt my throne above the stars of God: I will sit also upon the mount of the congregation, in the sides of the north: I will ascend above the heights of the clouds; I will be like the most High" (Isa. 14:12-14).

Not content with his exalted position as covering cherub, he aspired to be above all, even equal with God Himself.

Satan's unholy ambition led to the first war in the universe. "And there was war in heaven: Michael [Christ] and his angels fought against the dragon; and the dragon fought and his angels, and prevailed not; neither was their place found any more in heaven. And the great dragon was cast out, that old serpent, called the Devil, and Satan, which deceiveth the whole world: he was cast out into the earth, and his angels were cast out with him" (Rev. 12:7-9).

After Satan was cast out of heaven he and the angels who sided with him continued their rebellion on this earth. Satan caused the fall of our first parents and still carries on the warfare of evil against good that goes on in the human heart and all around us. "For we wrestle not against flesh and blood, but against principalities, against powers, against the rulers of the darkness of this world, against spiritual wickedness in high places" (Eph. 6:12).

The angels who remained loyal and true to God are helpful to man. They instruct, protect, and assist him in every way possible. Paul describes them in Hebrews 1:14: "Are they not all ministering spirits, sent forth to minister for them who shall be heirs of salvation?"

On the other hand, Satan and the angels who fell with him ("the angels that sinned," 2 Peter 2:4) endeavor to hold men in their rebellion against God and thus to keep them from attaining eternal life. He will use every means within his power, fair or foul, to accomplish his purpose.

Satan tempted Eve in the Garden of Eden. God had warned Adam and Eve that they should not eat of the tree of knowledge, the one and only tree that was forbidden. If they did, He told them, they would die. Satan countered with "Ye shall not surely die: for God doth know that in the day ye eat thereof, then your eyes shall be opened, and ye shall be as gods, knowing good and evil" (Gen. 3:4, 5).

God did not want them to know evil with all its baneful results, but Satan made it appear as though God was keeping from them something that would prove a great blessing. He deceived Eve and has been deceiving mankind ever since.

Satan used a serpent to beguile Eve. Of course, serpents cannot talk, but Eve heard this one speak. She was surprised and fascinated to have a snake converse with her, not realizing that it was the devil speaking through the first spiritist medium, a serpent. Satan has been using mediums ever since to deceive people.

Yes, the spirits are angels—evil angels. And they have the strength and power of angels. That is why they can do things that human beings cannot do. That is why they can perform miracles that mystify people.

In Matthew 4:5 we read, "Then the devil taketh him [Jesus] up into the holy city, and setteth him on a pinnacle of the temple." "Again, the devil taketh him up into an exceeding high mountain, and sheweth him all the kingdoms of the world, and the glory of them" (verse 8). Luke 4:5 adds, "in a moment of time." If Satan could literally take Christ bodily and set Him on the pinnacle of the Temple, and take Him up into a mountain and show Him all the kingdoms of the world in a moment of time, he has power beyond that of humans.

At times missionaries come in contact with persons possessed by demons. Pastor L. E. Tucker, of the Quiet Hour radio program, relates an experience that Pastor Edwardo Dingaosen had a month after he moved with his family to a pagan New Guinea village. One day, while Pastor Dingaosen was some distance away from the village, a messenger arrived with an urgent request that he return home. Arriving home, he found Sima, an 18-year-old village girl whom his wife had employed to help with the household duties, lying on her mat, terrified. The reason for her fear was that there were voices coming from her body. When Edwardo asked what was going on a deep voice answered, "We are spirits that have taken possession of this girl. We do not want her to study the Bible with you as she has been doing." They claimed that they were five spirits.

Earnestly Pastor Dingaosen and his wife prayed for the demons to depart, but they continued to torment the girl. Day after day they afflicted her and would not let her eat. Naturally this caused excitement in the village and people came to see her.

One villager asked the spirits if they had a leader. "Yes," came the answer. When asked the name of their leader, a husky voice replied, "His name is Lucifer."

Another asked where they came from.

"We were originally in Paradise," was the response. "But we chose to follow Lucifer and were cast out of heaven. For a time we went to other worlds, but now we spend all our time on earth. Wherever our leader tells us to go, we go."

Then they were asked if they were happy. Five voices almost shouted, "No!"

The spirits said they were going to leave Sima, but would be back with more spirits. The girl was thrown against the wall, but after a few minutes became normal. Then, for the first time in six days, she ate and began to recuperate from the terrifying experience of being controlled by demons.

Four days later she was thrown violently to the floor as evil spirits again took control of her body.

Pastor Dingaosen appointed a day of fasting and prayer and invited the villagers to come and witness the power of God. Joined by a few Christians from a neighboring village, Edwardo and his wife ate nothing all day or night and prayed constantly. As midnight approached, the spirit voices issuing from Sima's body began cursing. Then they cried, "We cannot stay longer. The good angels are too strong for us." Then there was peace. Sima had been delivered from the power of the devil. As a result, thirty-nine of the villagers became Christians, Sima among them.

Satan does have power, but he can go only so far, because God and the loyal angels have greater power than he.

When Jesus lived on earth He gave His disciples authority over evil spirits, to cast them out (Matt. 10:1; Mark 6:7; Luke 9:1). There is no reason to believe that He will not today honor with a similar authority those who genuinely seek to release others from Satan's bonds and to glorify His name.

"CHAINS YOU CAN NEVER BREAK"

One summer during my teen years some of my girl friends and I attended evangelistic meetings conducted in a tent not far from my home in Albany, New York.

Among the regular attendants was a woman who stood out from the rest. She was quite stout and wore a full, dark dress that hung loosely from her neck to her ankles. Her hair was drawn up tightly on top of her head, and on top of her hair was perched what was intended to be a hat, a small pill-box type of thing about six inches in diameter and three inches high. In her eyes was a faraway expression that added to her peculiar appearance. At the close of each meeting she would linger to talk to one or another of the evangelistic team.

I never met her personally then, but I saw her a few times downtown. Each time I saw her on the street I slipped into a store or hurried around a corner, like a typical teen-ager. I was afraid she would recognize me as one who attended the tent meetings, and speak to me. I didn't want anyone to think I knew "her."

On returning home from college a few years later, I was surprised to find that this woman was now a member of the church I attended. But how different she looked. She was neatly dressed, combed her hair in a becoming style, and wore an attractive hat. No longer was there that wild look in her eyes that made people uneasy in her presence. Instead, there was a kind, pleasant expression. I learned that she was Mrs. Whitney, an earnest Christian, and by now an officer in the church. What could have made such a difference?

Years later, when my husband was an ordained minister, Mrs. Whitney told us her story in the hope that he might be able to use it to help others interested or involved in spiritism.

When Mrs. Whitney got into spiritism she began to be guided by a spirit that she believed was the Holy Spirit. Deeper and deeper she plunged into the practice, until she was completely controlled by the spirit. It told her what food to buy, how to cook it, how and in what order to wash her dishes, how to arrange her home, and the procedure she should follow in doing her housework. It selected her clothes and told her how she should wear them—clothes that made her look as though she were demented.

But she was convinced that God was directing her.

One day the spirit told her, "There is one more thing you must do for me. Then you will be wholly mine. Tomorrow I want you to take a hatpin and pierce your eyes. Stand before the mirror and I will show you just how to stick the pin in your eyeballs. Then you will have obeyed me fully."

Mrs. Whitney got the hatpin and laid it on the dresser, all ready to use it on the morrow as the spirit directed, happy to know that then she would be wholly his.

That afternoon her daughter, a young woman, said, "Mother, you are so different since you are following the spirits."

"Different! How am I different? I am only obeying as the spirit guides me."

"You are different in every way and in everything you do. I used to love to bring my friends home and was proud to introduce you as my mother. Now I am really ashamed to have anyone know that you are my mother."

"How can you say that, Florence! You should love me even more because I am following the Lord."

"I can't help it, Mother. You dress differently; you act differently. Your face looks different."

She's ashamed of me! My child is ashamed of me! The mother was heartsick at Florence's words. But why should she be when I am doing everything the spirit tells me to do? People should see that I am growing more like Jesus. But she said she is ashamed of me, ashamed to let her friends know I am her mother!

These thoughts kept racing through her mind as she tried to grasp the import of her daughter's words.

She said I even look different! Going into her bedroom, Mrs. Whitney looked in the mirror. She couldn't see that she looked any different from what she had always appeared. But Florence said I look different, she thought.

She remained in front of her mirror staring at her own reflection. How was she different? Then, suddenly, she saw herself as her daughter, and others, must have seen her. The insight horrified her.

Do I really look like that? No wonder Florence is ashamed of me! Why should the Lord make me look this way? But—could it be that I am deceived? Oh, no!

"Who are you?" she demanded of the spirit.

"I am your guiding spirit." The answer came soothingly.

"Yes, I know. But who are you?"

"I told you I am your guiding spirit."

"But just who are you?"

"I'm your best friend."

"Are you the Holy Spirit?"

"No."

"Are you Jesus?"

"I told you I am your best friend."

"But are you Jesus Christ?"

"No!" the spirit snapped.

"No? Then who are you?"

"I said I am your guiding spirit." This time the answer came in a scream.

"In the name of Jesus Christ I command you to tell me who you are."

"*The devil.*"

To say that Mrs. Whitney was shocked is to put it mildly. She was unnerved, nearly crushed. To think that she had deeply believed she was being led by the Spirit of God and then to discover she was following the devil!

"Don't you try to get away from me!" the devil warned. "I have chains about you that you can never break."

Satan now began to do everything possible, it seemed, to harass her. He would trip her up or push against her as she walked. She would lie in her hammock in the yard, but he would dump her out on the ground. She never knew what was going to happen next.

It was about this time that the evangelist began his meetings in the tent. Disillusioned, and feeling the need of help, Mrs. Whitney went to the meetings. At the close of the first service she invited one of the team to visit her. But as she walked home the devil said, "He won't come to see you. You wait and see." And he was right.

Each evening, as she prepared to go to the tent, the spirit would say, "There's no use in your going to those meetings. They don't want you. They think you are crazy."

Each evening she would ask someone to come to see her. But the devil would say, "Why bother to ask them? They won't come."

During the day the devil pestered her and at night he would not let her sleep. If she did get to sleep he would rudely shake her to wake her up.

She tried to pray, but her prayers seemed to rise no higher than her head. "No need to pray," the spirit derided. "God has forsaken you. You are mine, and I will not let you go."

At other times he threatened. "I have chains about you that you can never break. If you try to get away from me, I will kill you."

The unfortunate woman felt desperate and almost hopeless. The tent meetings helped her, but no one from the meetings was visiting her. It seemed useless to pray. But she continued to go to the meetings and tried to pray, even though the spirit insisted that God had forsaken her.

Finally, one day as she was praying and pleading with God, after four long months of torture and anguish, heaven broke open and she knew her prayer had ascended to God. How wonderful! She knew God would help her. And He did!

In His strength she was able to break completely with spiritism. A defeated devil finally left her alone. She became a completely changed woman, in appearance and in every other way.

Mrs. Whitney was baptized and became a sincere, earnest church member and a faithful church worker until the time of her death.

Is it possible that a person can be serving Satan while thinking he is obeying the Lord? It would seem so. But if that person is totally sincere in seeking God's will, God will find ways of revealing His will to the individual.

Mrs. Whitney was honest at heart, but deceived. She was very grateful that God used her daughter to intervene just in time to save her from taking the irreversible step of destroying her eyesight.

THE WITCH OF ENDOR

What about the witch of Endor? Didn't she bring the prophet Samuel up from the dead? Doesn't this prove the dead can return?

You remember the story. King Saul, the first king of Israel, was losing the war against the Philistines, and needed help. So he at first went to God for help. But "when Saul enquired of the Lord, the Lord answered him not, neither by dreams, nor by Urim, nor by prophets" (1 Sam. 28:6).

Saul, proud and arrogant, had rebelled against God. Again and again the prophet Samuel had warned him to quit his evil ways, but he persisted in following his own course. He slew the priests of the Lord, sought to kill David, and rejected the counsel of Samuel until, by his stubbornness, he cut himself off from God.

Finally, the prophet was sent to deliver God's last message to the unfaithful king. In 1 Samuel 15:23 we read, "Because thou hast rejected the word of the Lord, he hath also rejected thee from being king." "And Samuel came no more to see Saul until the day of his death" (verse 35). Saul had sinned away his day of grace. God could do no more for him, so had to give him up.

Now, facing defeat at the hands of his enemies and realizing that God had forsaken him, the king turned in his desperation to one whom the Lord had commanded to be destroyed.

Israel had been bidden, "A man also or woman that hath a familiar spirit, or that is a wizard, shall surely be put to death" (Lev. 20:27). "Thou shalt not suffer a witch to live" (Ex. 22:18).

At an earlier time, in harmony with God's instruction, "Saul had put away those that had familiar spirits, and the wizards, out of the land" (1 Sam. 28:3). Now, hopeless and dejected, he commanded his servants, "Seek me a woman that hath a familiar spirit, that I may go to her, and enquire of her" (verse 7).

It was discovered that there was a witch living at a place called Endor, who had escaped the purge. Disguising himself so he would not be recognized, Saul went to visit her. The woman was afraid when she saw the kingly bearing of her visitor and said, "Behold, thou knowest what Saul hath done, how he hath cut off those that have familiar spirits, and the wizards, out of the land: wherefore then layest thou a snare for my life, to cause me to die?" (1 Sam. 28:9). Assuring her that no harm would befall her, Saul asked the witch to bring up Samuel.

"And the king said unto her, Be not afraid: for what sawest thou? And the woman said unto Saul, I saw gods ascending out of the earth" (1 Sam. 28:13); "I see a ghostly form coming up from the earth" (N.E.B.).

"And he said unto her, What form is he of? And she said, An old man cometh up; and he is covered with a mantle" (verse 14).

The undetailed description "an old man . . . covered with a mantle" was very little to go by. Certainly, it was no proof that it was Samuel. Moreover, the fact that Saul could not see the form itself but was only told what it was like, and made up his mind that it was Samuel ("And Saul perceived that it was Samuel") is hardly proof that it was the old prophet.

Notice that the witch did not see the old man come down from heaven, where, according to the popular belief, a dead prophet of God should have been. No, she saw the form "ascending out of the earth. . . . An old man cometh up." Moreover, the ghostly form complained, "Why hast thou disquieted me, to bring me up?" (verse 15). Even the spirit did not claim to come from heaven.

Saul himself admitted that God would no longer communicate with him by any of the channels He formerly used. "Saul answered, I am sore distressed; for the Philistines make war against me, and God is departed from me, and answereth me no more, neither by prophets, nor by dreams: therefore I have called thee" (verse 15).

Because Saul had committed the unpardonable sin and had been rejected by God, Samuel had been forbidden to see or speak to him during the remainder of his lifetime. Would the Lord permit His prophet, after he had died, to come to Saul at the bidding of a witch whom He had commanded to be put to death? If God would not communicate with the wicked king through his living prophet, would He communicate with him by the dead prophet at the command of a sorceress? God is consistent. The answer must be No.

In answer to the distressed king's question, What should I do? the supposed spirit of the dead Samuel said, "Tomorrow shalt thou and thy sons be with me" (verse 19).

The next day Israel was defeated in battle and Saul's three sons were killed. Wounded, and fearing to fall into the hands of the Philistines, Saul took his own life on the battlefield.

Samuel was a righteous prophet of God; Saul, because of his rebelliousness, was rejected of God. If the dead go to any other place than the grave, would they be together after death? Surely Saul would not go to heaven and certainly Samuel would not be in hell. So how could they be together in either of those places?

According to Bible teaching, the dead, good and bad, rich and poor, sleep in their graves. Because of his suffering, Job wished that he were dead. "For now should I have lain still and been quiet, I should have slept: then had I been at rest, With kings and counsellors . . . or with princes. . . . There the wicked cease from troubling; and there the weary be at rest. There the prisoners rest together . . . . The small and the great are there; and the servant is free from his master" (Job 3:13-19).

Ecclesiastes 3:20 says, "All go unto one place: all are of the dust, and all turn to dust again." They will rest together in their graves until the resurrection. Of the righteous person Jesus said, "I will raise him up at the last day" (John 6:40). So King Saul and his sons and the prophet Samuel are all in their graves and will remain there until the resurrection.

The record reads, "Saul died for his transgression which he committed against the Lord, even against the word of the Lord, which he kept not, and also for asking counsel of one that had a familiar spirit, to enquire of it; and enquired not of the Lord: therefore he slew him" (1 Chron. 10:13, 14).

So one of the reasons why God permitted Saul to die was that he consulted the witch of Endor. "And the soul that turneth after such as have familiar spirits, and after wizards, to go a whoring after them, I will even set my face against that soul, and will cut him off from among his people" (Lev. 20:6).

"Regard not them that have familiar spirits, neither seek after wizards, to be defiled by them. I am the Lord your God" (chap. 19:31).

"There shall not be found among you any ... that useth divination, or an observer of times, or an enchanter, or a witch. Or a charmer, or a consulter with familiar spirits, or a wizard, or a necromancer. For all that do these things are an abomination unto the Lord" (Deut. 18:10-12).

So it was not Samuel, the man of God, who appeared in response to the incantations of the witch, but an evil angel impersonating Samuel.

"When they shall say unto you, Seek unto them that have familiar spirits, and unto wizards that peep, and that mutter: should not a people seek unto their God? for the living to the dead? To the law and to the testimony: if they speak not according to this word, it is because there is no light in them" (Isa. 8:19, 20).

CAN THE SPIRITS PREDICT THE FUTURE?

We had the custom of spending a few days at Christmas time at my mother's home in Albany, New York. One year Elmer, my minister-husband, was conducting a series of evangelistic meetings in Keene, New York, three nights a week. One of his services would fall on Christmas night.

"I don't see how I can go down to Mother's this year," he reasoned. "I don't like to drop out a service now that the people are coming regularly." We talked it over and decided that I would go to Mother's for Christmas, and Elmer would come down after the service on Christmas night.

But as the time drew near, people said, "You can't hold a meeting on Christmas. No one would come. Everyone goes to the Methodist church that night." Keene was a small place with only three churches. Each year the Methodist church put on a big Christmas program, and everyone from miles around attended.

When my husband learned this he resolved to

drop out his service on Christmas night so all could attend the program at the Methodist church. He would go with me after all.

"Well, the spirits were wrong that time," Mother remarked on our arrival at her home.

"What do you mean?" we questioned.

"One evening about two weeks ago Bill and Ida [my brother and his wife] took me for a ride. It was so pleasant that we drove out in the country as far as Fred's place. During the evening, Fred, who is interested in spiritism, proposed that we have some fun with the spirits."

Mother continued to tell us the story. Fred asked questions, and the spirits would answer by rapping on the table. After a while he said, "Now, Aunt Mary, you ask something."

"I don't know what to ask," replied Mother.

"Ask anything; it doesn't matter."

"All right, then. Will Theresa be home for Christmas?"

"Yes," came the knocks on the table.

"Will Elmer be home?" Mother knew Elmer was holding meetings.

"No," came the answer.

"That's queer. If Theresa comes, Elmer will come also. Theresa doesn't drive. I didn't think they would be able to come this year, since one of his meetings would fall on Christmas night."

"Ask it again," advised Fred.

She did and the same answers came back. I

would be home but Elmer would not. But this time the rappings were louder.

"That surely can't be right. They would both come or neither would come," Mother insisted.

"Let me ask them," Fred suggested. "Will Theresa be home for Christmas?"

In reply the table pounded loudly, as though angry, "Yes."

"Will Elmer come also?" The table banged back the answer, "No!"

"So the spirits were wrong that time," Mother concluded.

We inquired the time she had been visiting Fred and learned it was at the very hour we had decided I should go home and Elmer would stay by and conduct his meeting.

We concluded that the reason the spirit could be so positive I would be home but not my husband was that it was aware of the decision we had just made. But it could not actually read the future to know that we would later change our minds. This suggested to us that Satan can know only so much about the future.

People wonder how fortunetellers often prove right in some of their predictions. For example, a person is told that he will be offered a new job. How could the fortuneteller or spiritualist know? Could we not understand that the devil or one of his fallen angels was present when the board or committee decided to offer the man the new job or promotion, so could foretell it through the medium?

Frequently fortunetellers inform their clients that they will receive a certain letter and, sure enough, in a day or two the letter arrives. We believe that a fallen angel saw that letter written, so knew about it, and used the fortuneteller to inform the recipient. By means such as this, people are wooed into spiritism.

We may also understand that Satan can manipulate circumstances so that he can cause certain events to take place.

Some predictions made by the spirits do not come true. Plans or decisions that may have been made by individuals are relayed by a spirit to a medium and passed on to an interested party. But changing circumstances cause the plans to be altered, so the predicted event does not occur, as our Christmas plans did not work out as first projected.

The devil has been studying human nature for thousands of years, so he can quite accurately surmise what a person will do under given circumstances. Even we can sometimes tell what a person is thinking by the expression on his face and other means. Knowing the characters and habits of the members of our family and close friends, we can frequently be reasonably sure what they will do under certain conditions.

In the book *Patriarchs and Prophets* it is put this

way: "Satan leads men to consult those that have familiar spirits; and by revealing hidden things of the past, he inspires confidence in his power to foretell things to come. By experience gained through the long ages, he can reason from cause to effect and often forecast, with a degree of accuracy, some of the future events of man's life. Thus he is enabled to deceive poor, misguided souls and bring them under his power and lead them captive at his will."—Page 687.

BODY, SOUL, AND SPIRIT

All will agree that the body rests in the tomb after death. But, the question is raised, does not the soul or spirit live on in an immortal state? This is a question that requires a Biblical answer.

The word *soul* appears some 530 times in the King James Version of the Bible. We discover that in the Old Testament it is, with only two exceptions, the translation of one Hebrew word. That word is translated by a number of other words in addition to soul.

Notice a few passages where we have the translation "soul": "And the Lord God formed man of the dust of the ground, and breathed into his nostrils the breath of life; and man became a living *soul*" (Gen. 2:7); "I said unto the children of Israel, No *soul* of you shall eat blood" (Lev. 17:12); "And they smote all the *souls* that were therein with the edge of the sword, utterly destroying them" (Joshua 11:11).

Sometimes the Hebrew word is translated "life" in the King James Version: "And God said, Let the waters bring forth abundantly the moving creature that hath *life*" (Gen. 1:20); "And it came to pass, when they had brought them forth abroad, that he said, Escape for thy *life*" (chap. 19:17).

"Person" is another way it is translated: "whosoever hath killed any *person*" (Num. 31:19; see also chap. 35:11, 15, 30).

It is also seen that the same Hebrew term translated as the above words, which refer to people, is used with reference to lower forms of life. For example, it is rendered "creature": "And God created great whales, and every living *creature* that moveth, which the waters brought forth abundantly" (Gen. 1:21; see also chap. 9:12, 15, 16).

In the New Testament "soul" is the rendering of only one Greek word. We have examples of its use in these texts: "Then they that gladly received his word were baptized: and the same day there were added unto them about three thousand *souls*" (Acts 2:41); "Behold my servant, whom I have chosen; my beloved, in whom my *soul* is well pleased" (Matt. 12:18).

The same Greek term is sometimes translated "life": "The Son of man came not to be ministered unto, but to minister, and to give his *life* a ransom for many" (Matt. 20:28); "Therefore I say unto you, take no thought for your *life*, what ye shall eat" (Luke 12:22).

At first thought the variety of words translated from the Hebrew and Greek terms—soul, creature, person, life, as well as some others in a few cases—may seem confusing. They may seem to have no common denominator. But when we look for a word that takes in each of these ideas, it seems that *individual*, or *individuality*, is that word. In most cases one of those words, or a modification of it, will fit the case. Try substituting one of them in the various texts we have quoted above. And, remember, there are *individual* fish, and birds, and so on, aren't there?

Now, notice something else: In one of the texts quoted we are told that "souls" can be killed. "And they smote all the souls . . . with the edge of the sword, utterly destroying them" (Joshua 11:11). Moreover, we read, "Behold, all souls are mine; as the soul of the father, so also the soul of the son is mine: the soul that sinneth, it shall die" (Eze. 18:4; see also verse 20).

Here are words of the Saviour: "And fear not them which kill the body, but are not able to kill the soul: but rather fear him [God] which is able to destroy both *soul* and body in hell" (Matt. 10:28).

We see, then, that the terms translated "soul," as used in the Bible, refer generally to the individual, or aspects of his individuality. And individuals can die, as we very well know, and as the Bible makes plain.

Now let us take a look at the word *spirit* as used in the King James Version of the Bible, with respect to man.

With only two exceptions the word *spirit* is translated from one Hebrew word. The same word is also rendered "breath" twenty-eight times. In addition, it is rendered as a few other words that do not relate to our study.

Examples of the translation "breath" are Job 12:10 and Psalm 146:4: "In whose [the Lord's] hand is the soul of every living thing, and the *breath* of all mankind"; "His [man's] *breath* goeth forth, he returneth to his earth; in that very day his thoughts perish."

Here are several examples in which the Hebrew word is translated "spirit": "All the while my breath is in me, and the *spirit* of God is in my nostrils" (Job 27:3); "He that hath no rule over his own *spirit* is like a city that is broken down, and without walls" (Prov. 25:28); "Who knoweth the *spirit* of man that goeth upward, and the *spirit* of the beast that goeth downward to the earth?" (Eccl. 3:21); "For thus saith the high and lofty One . . . I dwell . . . with him also that is of a contrite and humble spirit" (Isa. 57:15); "And it shall be [that] . . . every *spirit* shall faint, and all knees shall be weak as water" (Eze. 21:7).

In the New Testament of the King James

Version the term *spirit* is translated from one word, except in two cases. Typical examples of how the term is used with respect to men are: "And Mary said, . . . My *spirit* hath rejoiced in God my Saviour" (Luke 1:46, 47); "Now while Paul waited . . . at Athens, his *spirit* was stirred in him" (Acts 17:16); "They have refreshed my *spirit* and yours: therefore acknowledge ye them that are such" (1 Cor. 16:18); "But let it be the hidden man of the heart, . . . even the ornament of a meek and quiet *spirit*" (1 Peter 3:4).

An analysis of the Hebrew and Greek words translated "spirit" shows that the Hebrew word has the greater range of meaning, but that neither carries any hint of consciousness, or continuance of *life after death*. The Hebrew term suggests two applications, as may be seen by the texts quoted: (1) the vital principle, life force, sometimes represented by breath, and (2) the motivating power touching and energizing every phase of life. The latter meaning best fits the New Testament Greek term.

What does this suggest regarding what happens when a person dies?

In Ecclesiastes 12:7 we read, "Then shall the dust return to the earth as it was: and the spirit shall return unto God who gave it."

We need to recognize that we can only faintly have any understanding of what these words suggest. But they tell us that there is something that goes back to God. We have discovered that it is the vital principle, or life force. It might be described as the spark of life.

Perhaps this illustration will help us to understand what happens:

An electric light bulb by itself is cold and dark. But when the electricity is turned on and flows into it, it begins to glow and we have light. Similarly with man. Like the bulb, he was only a lifeless form until God gave him the principle of life, symbolized by, and accompanied by, breath. Man then became a living soul, person, or individual.

As it took a combination of the bulb and electricity to make light, so it took a combination of the physical body, formed of the elements of the earth, and the spirit of life to make a "soul" (Gen. 2:7).

Flick the switch controlling the electricity flowing to the bulb. The electricity no longer gets to the bulb, so the bulb goes dark, the light ceases to exist.

So, when the life principle, the spark of life from God, is no longer flowing to an individual, life ceases to exist. He has no life, as the light bulb has no light.

At this point it is instructive to notice that when Paul was talking to the Athenian philosophers about the true God, he said, literally,

"In Him we are living, and are being moved, and are existing." This tells us that our lives are dependent on Him moment by moment. In other words, the life principle comes from Him as continuously as the electricity flows to the burning light bulb.

IS MAN'S SOUL IMMORTAL?

What we discovered in the last chapter has partially answered the question we ask in this one, Is man's soul immortal? But let us examine the word *immortal* as it is used in the Bible, to discover whether scriptures will confirm what we have seen.

The word *immortal* is found only once in the King James Version of the Bible. It is applied to God. "Now unto the king eternal, *immortal*, invisible, the only wise God, be honour and glory forever and ever" (1 Tim. 1:17).

The word *immortality* is found five times in the King James Version. Here are the texts:

1 Timothy 6:15, 16: "Which in his times he shall shew, who is the blessed and only Potentate, the King of kings, and Lord of lords; *who only hath immortality.*" According to this, God is the only one who has immortality.

Romans 2:7: "To them who by patient continuance in well doing *seek for* glory and honour and *immortality*, eternal life." If we already possessed immortality we would not need to seek for it.

2 Timothy 1:10: "But is now made manifest by the appearing of our Saviour *Jesus Christ*, who hath abolished death, and hath *brought* life and *immortality* to light *through the gospel.*" Thus we *obtain* immortality by accepting the gospel of Jesus Christ.

The other two instances in which the term is used are found in 1 Corinthians 15:51-54: "Behold, I shew you a mystery; We shall not all sleep, but we shall all be changed. In a moment, in the twinkling of an eye, at the last trump: for the trumpet shall sound, and the dead shall be raised incorruptible, and we shall be changed. For this corruptible must put on incorruption, and *this mortal must put on immortality.* So when this corruptible shall have put on incorruption, and *this mortal shall have put on immortality*, then shall be brought to pass the saying that is written, Death is swallowed up in victory."

These texts, which are used in so many funeral services, are very plain. Mortal man will put on immortality and incorruption when the trumpet sounds and the dead are raised from their graves. That takes place when Jesus comes the second time.

The term *immortal soul* is not found in the Bible. So it is evident from the Scriptures that we do not naturally possess immortality. God only has immortality, but through accepting the gospel of Jesus Christ we may obtain immortality when the dead are resurrected and the living are translated at Christ's second coming. Immortality is a gift that God bestows upon those who serve Him, a gift that the wicked do not receive. "For the wages of sin is death; but the gift of God is eternal life through Jesus Christ our Lord" (Rom. 6:23).

Mrs. Reiswick and I were studying the Bible together on the subject of man's condition in death. I noticed that she was quite nervous when we began the study.

After I had shown her that the dead do not go to their rewards at death, but sleep in their graves until the resurrection, she breathed a sigh of relief and said, "I am so glad to know that—so glad the dead are asleep." Then she explained why she felt that way.

Sarah, one of her daughters, married a man who proved untrue to her and by his unfaithfulness contracted a social disease, which he passed on to her. Naturally, she was terribly upset and worried. At that time there was no real cure for the disease. She was very afraid that her two small children might become infected, and this preyed on her mind.

One morning, after Sarah had visited her mother, she went home, sealed all the doors and windows, and turned on the gas.

Like most people, Mrs. Reiswick had been taught that the dead go either to heaven or to hell at death. She had read the words of Revelation 22:15: "For without are dogs, and sorcerers, and whoremongers, and murderers . . ."

The last thing Sarah did was to commit murder by killing herself. A murderer could be forgiven and saved if he repented, but how could her daughter repent? So the mother believed that since her darling child could not go to heaven, she must be in hell.

"You have no idea what I have gone through during these two years since Sarah died," Mrs. Reiswick told me. "I have heard ministers describe hell and the awful anguish suffered by the lost souls who go there. I could picture my daughter in that dreadful place, burning, burning. And I believed it would never end, that she would have to suffer on and on forever and ever. That picture has been continually before me and has almost driven me out of my mind.

"You will never know what reading those texts from the Bible has done for me," she continued. "What a relief to know that Sarah is not burning in hell now, that she is not in agony, but is peacefully sleeping in her grave! What terrible dreams, sleepless nights, and agonizing days I might have been spared had I only known that before."

Our heavenly Father looks down with sympathy and pity upon one mourning the loss of a loved one who was not righteous, and He offers comfort through the knowledge that the deceased is quietly resting in the grave, not writhing in anguish of hell.

There are two resurrections brought to view in the Bible, a thousand years apart. "Marvel not at this: for the hour is coming, in the which all that are in the graves shall hear his voice, and shall come forth; they that have done good, unto the resurrection of life; and they that have done evil, unto the resurrection of damnation" (John 5:28, 29).

The first resurrection, which is only of the righteous, takes place at the second coming of Christ. "The Lord himself shall descend from heaven with a shout, with the voice of the archangel, and with the trump of God: and the dead in Christ shall rise first: Then we [who are true Christians] which are alive and remain shall be caught up together with them in the clouds, to meet the Lord in the air: and so shall we ever be with the Lord" (1 Thess. 4:16, 17).

"Blessed and holy is he that hath part in the first resurrection: on such the second death hath no power, but they shall be priests of God and of Christ, and shall reign with him a thousand years" (Rev. 20:6).

So the righteous dead are resurrected and

taken to heaven when Jesus comes, "but the rest of the dead lived not again until the thousand years were finished" (Rev. 20:5). The unrighteous dead do not receive their rewards at Christ's return, but a thousand years later, at the close of the millennium. Then they are called from their graves to receive their recompense. What is that? "Fire came down on them from heaven and consumed them" (Rev. 20:9, N.E.B.).

Thus, according to the Word of God, the wicked do not spend eternity in a burning hell. There is a burning hell brought to view in the Scriptures, but in the fire of that hell sinners are "consumed." Revelation 20:14 calls this "the second death."

Describing this destruction of the wicked, the prophet Malachi wrote: "The day that cometh shall burn them up, saith the Lord of hosts, that it shall leave them neither root nor branch. ... For they shall be ashes under the soles of your feet in the day that I shall do this, saith the Lord of hosts" (Mal. 4:1, 3). And, in 2 Thessalonians 1:9 we read that they "shall be punished with everlasting destruction," but they are not suffering now. It might be noted that the text says "destruction," which is a state, and suggests completion. It does not suggest a process of destroying.

So there are two sides to the picture. It might be comforting to think of our departed loved ones basking in the beauties and joys of heaven. But it would not be so pleasant to think of those who were not righteous writhing in the fires of hell year after burning year. No, our God is merciful and in His loving compassion He permits both good and bad to rest in sleep in their graves until the resurrection, when they will receive their rewards.

11

SPIRITISM IS NOT CHRISTIAN

One day when I was just a girl, Cousin Fred, who was much older than I, dropped by our home for a visit. Fred, who had recently become interested in spiritism, explained to Mother and me how he talked with the spirits, who answered him by knocking on the table. He was very enthusiastic about his supposed communications with the dead.

He also told us that his son, who was just a toddler, had an invisible playmate. The youngster visited with his unseen friend and played with him just as he would with a real boy. He even knew his name.

However, Fred said something that perturbed me so much that I never again felt quite the same toward him. He stated that Jesus was a good man, but only a man. He did not accept Him as the divine Son of God. To me Jesus was just what He claimed to be, God's only-begotten Son, and the Saviour.

Years ago, a writer asserted in *The Progressive Thinker,* a leading journal of spiritism, "While we gladly accept many beautiful things as taught by Christ, we cannot afford to call ourselves Christian, for that would imply that we believe his blood really cleanses from sin, and we deny that."

The author continued, "I denounce the following: the vicarious atonement, the doctrine of eternal punishment, the literal resurrection of the body, the virgin birth of Jesus, the infallibility of the Bible, the doctrine of salvation by faith only. No, the Spiritualist religion is as different from the so-called Christian religion as a sunny day is from a starless night."

The crux of the matter is this: Are we going to accept the teachings of spiritism or those of the Bible as being true and authoritative? If we accept the Bible as being right, we cannot possibly believe in spiritism.

Let us see how this is.

If Jesus is not the divine Son of God, then the Bible is a false book. For throughout the Old Testament is a thread of prophecy leading to a coming Messiah. The writers of the Gospel weave this thread into a pattern that pictures Jesus exactly, and the other New Testament authors interweave their writings with the same pattern. Therefore, if Jesus is not the prophesied Messiah the Bible becomes a discredited book.

Paul warns in 1 Timothy 4:1 that "in the latter

times some shall depart from the faith, giving heed to seducing spirits, and doctrines of devils." And in 2 John 7 we read, "For many deceivers are entered into the world, who confess not that Jesus Christ is come in the flesh. This is a deceiver and an antichrist."

Jesus claimed to be the Christ. When conversing with the woman of Samaria about the Messiah, "which is called Christ," He replied, "I that speak unto thee am he" (John 4:25, 26).

Jesus' disciples accepted Him as God's Son. Speaking for the other apostles, Peter declared, "We believe and are sure that thou art that Christ, the Son of the living God" (chap. 6:69).

On two occasions the Holy Father Himself acknowledged in an audible voice Jesus of Nazareth as His Son. After Christ's baptism "a voice [came] from heaven, saying, This is my beloved Son, in whom I am well pleased" (Matt. 3:17). On the Mount of Transfiguration God again spoke the same words and added, "Hear ye him" (Matt. 17:5).

The devils recognized and acknowledged Him. On one occasion Jesus and His disciples came upon two men possessed by devils. Speaking through the men the demons cried out, saying, "What have we to do with thee, Jesus, thou Son of God?" (Matt. 8:29).

The Bible gives various tests whereby we may ascertain whether the spirits are true or false. The most important of them are:

Test them by the Word of God. "To the law and to the testimony: if they speak not according to this word, it is because there is no light in them" (Isa. 8:20). Spiritists do not teach in harmony with the Scriptures. As we have seen, they reject such doctrines of the Bible as the divinity of Jesus, the infallibility of the Bible, the fall of Satan, the virgin birth, the atonement, and the resurrection. If any supernatural being appears to you, even though he appears as an angel of light—and Paul warns that Satan himself will come as such a being (2 Cor. 11:14)—we should test it on this basis. If it fails to acknowledge these teachings as being true, we may be assured that this is not of God.

Question their attitude toward Jesus Christ. If they do not confess that Jesus was the Messiah, including everything that teaching implies, they are false spirits.

"Every spirit that confesseth that Jesus Christ is come in the flesh is of God: and every spirit that confesseth not that Jesus Christ is come in the flesh is not of God: and this is that spirit of antichrist, whereof ye have heard that it should come" (1 John 4:2, 3).

Challenge them in the name of Jesus Christ. You remember that when Mrs. Whitney commanded the spirit in the name of Jesus Christ, it obeyed her.

You will also remember that on one occasion Paul was preaching in a Greek city called Philippi, when a young girl that had a "spirit of divination" (Acts 16:16) began to pester him. "And this did she many days. But Paul, being grieved, turned and said to the spirit, I command thee in the name of Jesus Christ to come out of her. And he came out the same hour" (verse 18).

"Resist the devil, and he will flee from you" (James 4:7).

The Bible is truth. The Bible is the Word of God. And all who fully follow that Word find peace, happiness, and release from guilt and fear. They find freedom in Him who said, "If the Son therefore shall make you free, ye shall be free indeed" (John 8:36).

In spiritism there may at the beginning appear to be light, knowledge, power, happiness. There may be excitement, adventure, a satisfaction in delving into the mysterious. But it is a tunnel going underground, a tunnel that has no opening at the other end, only blackness forever. Spiritism is of the devil. Therefore avoid it. Your eternal destiny depends on your making that decision.

www.ingramcontent.com/pod-product-compliance
Lightning Source LLC
Chambersburg PA
CBHW060533030426
42337CB00021B/4243

(bitter) Sweet Nothings

written and illustrated by Tina G.

(bitter) Sweet Nothings by Tina G.
Published by Geez Louise Publishing

© 2017 Tina G.

All rights reserved. No portion of this book may be reproduced in any form without permission from the publisher, except as permitted by U.S. copyright law.

For permissions contact:

GeezLouisePublishing@gmail.com

Cover and artwork by Tina G.

ISBN: 978-0-9994970-0-5

For the love of my life:

I am the adjective,
you are the noun;
I was put here on earth
to describe you

TABLE OF CONTENTS

Foreword	9
The Sweet	11
The Bitter	33
The Rest	65

FOREWORD: A SALESMAN'S PITCH

I could sell you
a nickel for a dime
a love for a time,
tindered love and care
for us to share,
you won't even notice
I'm only half there.

And what's a
transaction sans action?
I'll sell you that too,
make you fall for that too;
money can't buy happiness
but look here, look what buying
my love can do for a
sweet, sweet girl
like you...

The Sweet

We met in an inbox
and the walls
closed in on me

world collapsed
into an iPhone 5s screen

swirls of you and blue
light up my nights—

I can't sleep,
it's you that I need.

We are so…. idk. vast

you make it safe
to open up and I find
myself boundless

it's so easy to build
a world with you,
who says we need
to share space?

I love the way we think around each other, sweet minds twisting into knots that can't be tugged apart. You'd have to cut yourself free when the time came, leaving a bit of yourself behind, taking a bit of me with you.

You rise in my skies every morning;
I wake up in awe of such light

I revel in rays of attention,
I bask in the heat you ignite.

I reach out but you won't come closer,
for fear I'll be engulfed in flame;

I've already lived below freezing,
now burning away is my aim.

Tell me what you're thinking,
let me in on what you need…
teach me your language
so I can love you in it

THE AIRPORT PARKING LOT

I still remember when we finally
saved enough between us for a visit
and I picked you up once your plane
touched down, remember?

We'd kissed and kissed and kissed
and kissed some more and

I kept spoiling it by smiling too widely
to keep them unbroken
but you didn't seem to mind

since my lips, like my mind,
always returned to you
before long

the honey is sweeter
when you love the bee

I can tell you anything and
you can tell me all of you;
our skeletons polished
to a high shine,
look at us,
a couple of
closet romantics.

LONG DISTANCE

At first loving you was like
owning a star; the receipt
didn't mean within reach

now it's like owning the stadium:
look at you closely, you'll see
signs of me everywhere

touch may be rare but my words
have always been my intimacy

I use my tongue to etch
myself into your surface,

each laugh we share
is how I plant my flag.

I am a puzzle with
handfuls of pieces
that keep turning up
in your pockets;
I pray you are here
to complete me.

The
Bitter

It can't be as fun as
you make it out to be,
splitting your heart
into pieces and juggling them,
letting some fall
into the wrong hands
when I'm the only one
you need to hold onto.

Let the away teams play
all the mind games

honey,
I'M home.

My love is an angry little thing,
complex Napoleon dynamite
I'll self-destruct before
you're halfway out
the door

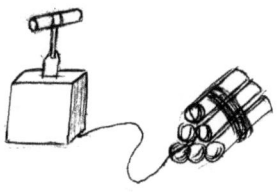

SACRILEGIOUS

You kept her a secret
to 'save' me from hurt feelings

a true o-missionary; how heroic
but who were you saving?

The truth is always laid bare, always there
to make martyrs of women like me

that's why when I said we were through,
part of me died too.

You snuck inside
and changed the locks,
became the key,
and then got lost.

HIS

You creep into my poetry
uninvited, inevitable.

The ghost of your touch
guides my pen and
the tempting lips
of your phantom
help shape my words;

I find it selfish,
the way I'm used
to tell your story.

AND HERS

When you became mine,
I assumed you were no longer
yours to give away

If you were wondering,
my life was perfectly fine
before I chose you.
It's kind of funny when you
think about it, that I
wrote my own ending,
carved my own hell out in the
shape of your silhouette,
eternal resting place,
I can't sleep without you.

You've always been the rose,
anyone with eyes can see that;
does that make me the concrete
you broke through to grow?

FOOTNOTE[1]

1. such solemn saints,
martyrs of moonlit revelry,

sacrificed every seven days
to resurrect a confidence

six inches high.

DETOX

I have no idea
what I'm doing here,
but I know what
I'm running from

watch me spike
some tall glass of water
with lemon

watch me
sweat you out
at his hands

I usually paid for my own drinks
but that night he picked up the tab,

slid the bills slid across the counter
with a quick *I'll handle this*
and I didn't argue; the fight
in me was gone, it felt good
to give in.

Something about him
drained me in a good way, made my
white flag wave hello each time
he crossed my borders

his kiss seemed to say *drop your weapons, no need
to wage war right this second, you could do
with some refuge.*

He was peace, a sweet olive branch romance
but I was caged in nostalgia
and lost in thought, reliving
time spent under fire.

I pay so much attention to
who sweeps me off my feet
that I tend to overlook
who picks me up
and dusts me off

Yeah he's sweet
but what's the point,

what's a band-aid
to a stab wound,

I'm just gonna
bleed right
through

UNEMPLOYMENT LINE

It didn't take me long to
send him here and I regret it;

his heart was overqualified
and mine was never in it.

He gave me all his time, hope he
finds better ways to spend it.

What can I say?
You're a hurdle,
and I can't
get over it.

The Rest

DEATH OF A SALESMAN

So you're just
gonna stroll up,
tip your hat to
heaven's gates

and ask if she'll
let you in again?

just like that?

just like that.

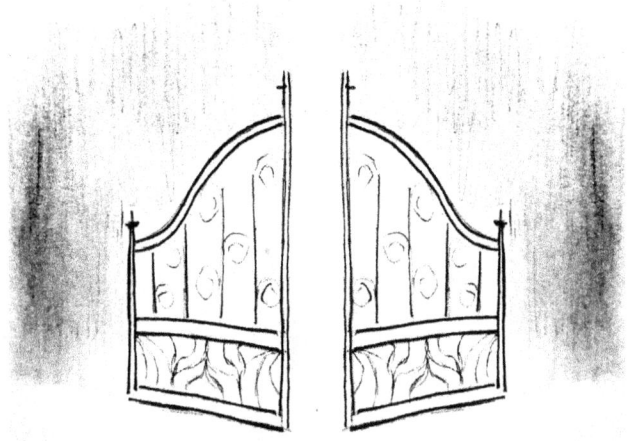

BOOKMARKED

For the record, I hate
that you know me so well,
I hate that I still hold your place,
I hate that I love you so much,
just enough
to let you back in,
again and again.

(9TH) LIFE LESSON

Your arms sting from
the marks I left after
clawing my way out
of your embrace
yet again

but who's really
to blame here…

the same hands that
held my head under water
the last eight times I drowned
now reach for me

forgive me if I flinch.

Forgiving you is no easy task;
logic and ration only go so far,
it still smarts.

Her name on your lips
is like a needle prick;

I look past your eyes
brimming with memories
and see her right there,
under your skin.

sometimes I worry
my lack of sharp edges
means I haven't pierced through,
means I'm not there too.

Flipped through my journal yesterday
and finally realized

each entry was a love letter
to you, to my surprise.

Good thing then, that you're someone new,
someone I've never met,

someone who reads me loud and clear,
someone who's writing back.

ROUGH DRAFT

---

grab your favorite pen
and doodle all in my margins

try to erase my worry lines
and take notes on my reactions

underline my underlying concerns
and make your solutions bold

trace your name on my skin in cursive

but write your intentions in print
so I can't misread them

follow my directions and I promise I'll
scratch out your past mistakes

and circle you in bright red ink
to let you know you've finally earned

100% of me

MY LOVE:

we've been gifted
with a second chance,
a whole new slew of firsts

this time will be better,
this time we will
grow up together.

guess that makes us
childhood sweethearts?
fitting, considering

when we first met, my
soul knew I'd known
you forever.

even after we fade into nothing,
this will have been
everything

ABOUT THE AUTHOR

Tina G. holds a B.A. in Economics from NC A&T SU. She works in Project Management and resides in NC with her fiancé. This book was a labor of love, and she loves her job.

To learn more about Tina, visit www.tinagworks.com.

www.ingramcontent.com/pod-product-compliance
Lightning Source LLC
Chambersburg PA
CBHW060530030426
42337CB00021B/4205